917.55
N55t

90116

DATE DUE			

THE
TOWN OF FINCASTLE
VIRGINIA

THE
TOWN OF FINCASTLE
VIRGINIA

Frances J. Niederer
Hollins College, Virginia

The University Press of Virginia
Charlottesville

Copyright © 1965 by the Rector and Visitors
of the University of Virginia

The University Press of Virginia

First published 1965

Second printing 1966

Library of Congress
Catalog Card Number: 65–26013
Printed in the United States of America

ACKNOWLEDGMENTS

COLLABORATING with me in the initial study of Fincastle were Ruth Shipe Monk, Pattie Holmes Petrou, and Betsy Speer Taylor; to each of them I am deeply grateful. I also wish to thank warmly all those residents of Fincastle and Botetourt County who so generously opened their homes and churches to us and shared with us their knowledge of the town. It is impossible to name them all, but for help given freely and frequently I thank Miss Rebekah Peck, Mr. Taylor Peck, Mrs. William M. Simmons, Mr. and Mrs. Robert D. Stoner, and Mr. and Mrs. Roy E. Bolton. I am equally indebted to the Roanoke Historical Society, particularly to Dr. Margaret P. Scott, Mr. Edmund P. Goodwin, and Mr. George Kegley, for advice and encouragement. For plans and photographs I thank Mr. Jack Gaking, Mr. John W. Lawrence, and Mr. James M. Yeatts.

The Virginia State Library kindly made available tax lists, newspapers, and insurance policies and has given permission to include as part of this text an article published in *Virginia Cavalcade*. The libraries of the University of Virginia were most helpful in providing newspapers and architectural handbooks, as was the National Trust for Historic Preservation in providing building plans.

I also wish to express my appreciation to Hollins College for financial assistance in the preparation and publication of this study.

F. J. N.

CONTENTS

ILLUSTRATIONS

PLANS

THE
TOWN OF FINCASTLE
VIRGINIA

FINCASTLE: THE FIRST
FIFTY YEARS

I

THE pioneers coming down the Great Valley of Virginia along old
Indian trails in the years just after the Revolution must have been eager
to reach the new frontier town of Fincastle, last outpost before the great
wilderness. Would this, perhaps, be where they would take up land,
build their houses, establish their families and their businesses? Was
this where they would enjoy the rights and privileges of free Ameri-
cans, in the shadow of the new Botetourt courthouse?

Already, miles from town, they were seeing men repairing old roads,
surveying for new ones, building bridges. They were passing farms
with fertile soil, lush pasturage, fine two-story houses; seeing many
mills in use and more being constructed; noting an occasional ordinary.
Finally, as they followed Miller's Creek and turned up the slight rise
east of the mill there, they found themselves in the clearing before the
courthouse itself. Here was a cluster of dwellings and stores—lumber
store, saddler's shop, ordinaries—stretched out along the wide street
that led to the town spring two blocks away. At the top of the hill above
the spring was the lot set aside for an Episcopal church. It was perhaps
even then being built.

Almost two centuries have passed since then, but time has gone
slowly in the Valley. The pattern of its rolling hills, its meadows and

little streams, its prairies and forests, rests basically unchanged. The town of Fincastle, twenty miles northeast of the city of Roanoke, has spread a little, but not far. Its streets are paved, but they are the same wide and shady streets laid out under County Surveyor William Preston in 1770.[1] Walking along them one can easily find the town spring in its picturesque hollow, the courthouse common, the church-yard with its beautiful vista over wooded hills to the north.

The town of Fincastle was founded and named in 1772, when the act establishing it was passed by the Virginia General Assembly. The name honored George Lord Fincastle, son of Lord Dunmore, Lieutenant Governor of Virginia, whose family property in Perthshire, Scotland, included the site of an old fort named Fincastle.[2] The settlement in Virginia, known as Botetourt Courthouse, was two years old at the time and growing fast.

Settlers had been coming to this area of southwestern Virginia for some three or four decades. The land grant of 92,100 acres, including 8,100 acres on Catawba Creek, which was made to Benjamin Borden in 1739, was the first of several large grants in the area from which smaller units were almost immediately made available to settlers.[3] First-generation Scotch or Scotch-Irish immigrants dominated in the beginning; they numbered half of the company of fifty-two Rangers for the Catawba and Roanoke valleys in 1755.[4] But soon German families, and some German-Swiss, began to come in numbers, many moving down from the northern counties of Virginia or, like the Scotch-Irish, down from Pennsylvania. Settlers also came from eastern Virginia and Mary-land, many of these of English birth or parentage, and there was a sprinkling of French, Irish, Dutch, and Welsh.[5]

The pioneer society was of course an agricultural one. Of the crops set out, hemp was the most important because of the demand for it by

---

[1] Lewis P. Summers, *Annals of Southwest Virginia, 1769–1800* (Abingdon, Va., 1929), p. 61.

[2] F. B. Kegley, *Kegley's Virginia Frontier* (Roanoke, Va., 1938), pp. 404–5.

[3] For detailed accounts of settlements, see Kegley, pp. 53ff., and Robert D. Stoner, *A Seed-Bed of the Republic* (Roanoke, Va., 1962), pp. 13ff.

[4] See Stoner, pp. 79–81, and Kegley, p. 212, for replicas of the roster, which gives us a sample of provenances. Twenty-four Rangers list Ireland as their country, 12 England, 3 Germany, 8 Pennsylvania, 2 Virginia, 1 Jersey, 1 New England, 1 Scotland. The Scotch-Irish, who had come to Pennsylvania in large numbers in 1717–18 and again in 1725–29, came to the Shenandoah Valley particularly after the famine in Ireland in 1740–41. For details of this and later migrations of the eighteenth century, see James G. Leyburn, *The Scotch-Irish* (Chapel Hill, N.C., 1962), pp. 172ff., 204ff.

[5] Stoner, pp. 22–23, 31–32, 360.

British shipping, and, judging from the Fincastle court records of 1770–71, everyone was growing hemp.[6] Next largest crops were wheat and corn, and early there were many mills. Settlers came with varied skills: among the 1755 Rangers, for example, there were three weavers, three tailors and one button maker, two coopers, two millwrights and three carpenters, two distillers, and one surgeon. The establishment of the town and courthouse naturally attracted merchants and lawyers and encouraged the setting up of various trades.[7]

Most of the preliminary planning for Fincastle was done in the spring of 1770. The new county of Botetourt had been formed after the division of Augusta in November, 1769.[8] Of its thirteen justices, appointed in December by His Majesty's Commission of the Peace at Williamsburg, eight were Scotch-Irish, one was French, and the others were English or perhaps Welsh.[9] The justices held their first monthly meeting from February 13 to 15, 1770. There were already a good many houses at Miller's Mill, center of the new county, and Israel Christian donated 45 acres of land to serve as nucleus for a town. Two and a half acres of this were set aside for a courthouse site and ten acres for prison bounds. The rest was laid out in half-acre lots to be sold, and there was no lack of purchasers.[10]

Much had to be done that spring of 1770. Plans for the courthouse and jail were decided upon at the April meeting. The court ordered that an agreement be made with a workman "to build a log cabbin twenty four feet long and twenty feet wide for a Court House, with a clapbord roof with two small sheads, one at each end for jury rooms."[11] The designation "log cabbin" is notable, for this is the earliest known use of the term. It apparently was a Scotch-Irish invention, to make clear that the justices wanted a sturdier structure than the Irish "cabin" with which many of them were familiar.[12]

Building of the courthouse was delayed for three years. But a jail and stocks had to be built at once, to carry out the instructions of His

[6] Summers, pp. 75–79; Kegley, pp. 391–92.

[7] See Stoner, pp. 46ff., for a discussion of agriculture and stock raising and, pp. 36ff., for industries.   [8] Kegley, p. 377.

[9] Andrew Lewis, William Preston, John Maxwell, James Trimble, and George Skillern had been born in Ireland, Israel Christian on the Isle of Man, and William Fleming in Jedburgh. Representing the second generation in America were Robert Breckenridge (Scotch-Irish), John Bowyer (English), and Benjamin Estill (French, born d'Estelle). Richard Woods, David Robinson (who had come from Pennsylvania), and Benjamin Hawkins were probably English, or perhaps Welsh (Stoner and Kegley, passim).

[10] Summers, pp. 66, 77, 79–80.   [11] Ibid., p. 77.

[12] Harold R. Shurtleff, The Log Cabin Myth (Cambridge, Mass., 1939), pp. 25–26.

Majesty's Commission of the Peace to "punish the offenders and breakers" of laws and court orders.[13] James McGavock, undersheriff of the county, was given the construction contract, with orders "to build a log cabin twenty feet long and sixteen feet wide, with an addition at the end of it the same width and twenty feet long for a prison and the Gaoler's House."[14] By May stocks had been erected, and by August the jail had been finished except for the locks, which had to be imported. Later there was added a public ducking stool, presumably in the millpond a block away from the prison.[15]

Both prison and stocks seem to have taken hard use, for there are many entries in court orders during the 1770's and 1780's concerning their repair or replacement. An order of August, 1777, called for a completely new and stronger jail, "of square loggs at least fourteen inches square, floured both above and below of loggs of the same dimentions, and the roof to be of lapt joint shingles."[16] It may be that the court had in mind a structure like that of the pioneer fort houses: large, closely set logs, dovetailed at the corners.[17] It was not until 1779 that this new prison was ready; the builders, Jasper Robinet and Thomas McClure, were so slow that the court had to threaten to bring suit against them to get the building finished.[18]

The courthouse was finished in August of 1773, except for locks and bolts which were procured some time later. Its cost was 435 pounds 10 shillings and 9 pence, an amount paid off over a long period of years to the builder, Robert Clark.[19] Like the prison, the courthouse was frequently repaired, and by 1798 it may have been completely rebuilt. The plan of this later structure, shown on Matthew Harvey's insurance policy for his house across the street, indicates that it was a simple square building with walls of lumber instead of log. Unfortunately its dimensions are not given.[20]

What about the dwellings in the early town? A listing about 1784 of homeowners in and near Fincastle gives us a good indication of the types of houses.[21] Among the 59 buildings listed, there are 26 "log dwelling houses," 21 "cabins to dwell in" plus 1 "duble cabin," and 11 "frame dwelling houses."

Obviously the "cabins to dwell in" were temporary shelters. The list

---

[13] Summers, p. 59.   [14] Ibid., p. 77.   [15] Ibid., pp. 81, 91, 411.
[16] Ibid., p. 265.
[17] See photographs of Garst Fort House on Carvin's Creek in Kegley, pp. 516–17.
[18] Summers, p. 280.   [19] Ibid., p. 200; Stoner, p. 178.
[20] Mutual Assurance Society Against Fire on Buildings of the State of Virginia (established December 26, 1795), Policy No. 29 (filed in Virginia State Library, Richmond as are all the insurance policies cited in this chapter).   [21] Stoner, pp. 233–35.

specifically mentions the number and the material of chimneys for the other buildings, but not one of these cabins has a chimney. They were the common pioneer huts of saplings or untrimmed logs, crudely calked and roofed with split staves held down by poles, and with earthen floors.[22] An appraisal of "work and improvements" on a tract of land in Fincastle County made for George Washington in 1775 gives us their normal size, 12 by 12 feet, and their slight value, five pounds.[23]

Some cabins, of course, were less primitive than these. Dr. Doddridge's account of the erection of a better one (for a newly married couple) gives us a vivid picture of the procedure followed.[24] During the first day a group of choppers felled the trees, cut them into proper lengths, and assorted them at the site for the sides and ends of the cabin. "A carpenter, if such he might be called," sought a proper tree, "straight-grained, and from three to four feet in diameter," from which the clapboards for the roof were split. Meanwhile another group of men were "splitting trees about 18 inches in diameter, and hewing the faces of them with a broad-axe" for the puncheons for the cabin floor. The second day the walls were raised, with four "corner-men" elected "to notch and place the logs." As the walls rose, laying of the floor was begun, and openings were cut and strengthened for door and chimney. Finally the clapboards of the roof were put in place. Then during the third day the floor was leveled and some furniture was built in. Meanwhile, masons prepared billets to chink the cracks, daubed them in place with mortar, and with "a few stones formed the back and jambs of the chimney."

The "duble cabin" listed in 1784 is exceptional in having two stone chimneys. One surmises that there were here both better structure and a plan of the "possum-trot" or "dogrun" type, that is, a cabin having two rooms separated by a roofed breezeway, with an end chimney in each room.[25]

[22] Shurtleff, p. 27.   [23] Summers, p. 671.

[24] The Rev. Dr. Joseph Doddridge's account is included in Samuel Kercheval's *History of the Valley of Virginia,* first published in 1833. In the third edition (Woodstock, Va., 1902), it is on pp. 270–71.

[25] For plans and photographs of cabins of this type, which apparently originated in Virginia and spread to North Carolina, see F. B. Johnston and T. T. Waterman, *The Early Architecture of North Carolina* (Chapel Hill, N.C., 1941), pp. 7, 16, 19. Quoted here is part of their description: "In the Dog-Run house two separate, identical buildings were constructed side by side, about ten feet apart, and were covered by one roof that also spanned the passageway. This scheme produced a useful pioneer dwelling, one room of which was the bedroom, and the other the kitchen and living room, while the covered passage formed a place for household activities in summer and a cool place for the family to sit on warm evenings. The passage was also used for curing pelts and storing traps in winter, and was a sheltered place for hunting dogs" (p. 7).

The largest group listed in 1784 is that of the "log dwelling houses." German and German-Swiss immigrants had been erecting copies of their native log houses in Pennsylvania, and the Scotch-Irish had quickly adopted them.[26] Among the 26 log dwellings described in the Fincastle list, twelve had stone chimneys; limestone is common in the area. Eight had clay chimneys and two had brick. Roofs were shingled.

There remain in Fincastle a few of the small log houses which once clustered in the area around the town spring, a public site for water supply since Indian days, and we may take Miss Mary Peck's house on the corner of Carper Street as typical of the simplest plan. This tiny house (16 by 20 feet) was only recently covered with clapboards, and in the attic one can still see rough-cut logs and an original casement window. In the early days the single room on the ground floor was divided into living and sleeping quarters by a wooden partition and a curtain. In one end wall there was a large fireplace. At the other end

[26] Shurtleff, pp. 175–76; Charles M. Stotz, *The Early Architecture of Western Pennsylvania* (Pittsburgh, Pa., 1936), photographs on pp. 36–38, 40–42.

2   Peck House

there was a small dugout for storage of food, and over this a narrow ladder led to the loft in which the children slept.[27] Similar construction was used in two houses on Back Street between Monroe and Hancock: the old potter's shop and the Becky Holmes house. Both of these were originally one story high and small; they have been changed considerably. The Holmes house retains its original basement, with its low ceiling resting on bark-covered logs, and its large fireplace. Town legend holds that Israel Christian built this house and that he later gave it to his slaves, the Holmeses. Supposedly the first Negro church services in Fincastle were held here.

Although dwellings with exposed-log walls are no longer visible in Fincastle, several examples may be found a few miles from the town. These are now again inhabited, with surprisingly few modifications other than modern utilities.

One of the best preserved of these is the present Selander house on county route 630.[28] Typically, it stands in a valley, next to a spring which has never run dry. This two-storied house, probably built about 1800, was of the possum-trot type. From the breezeway, centered doors led to the downstairs rooms, and there was a front entrance just to the left of the present door. Narrow winding staircases tucked into room corners led to the upper floor. The attached back extension, added later, had its own staircase to an upper room. The breezeway has recently been enclosed and a staircase built within it, but it still has part of its original roof. (The windows are not the original ones.) In this house the roughly hewn oak logs are joined at the corners in Pennsylvania-German style, with gable-cut log ends fitted under broad-angled notches. The wide spaces left between the logs are filled with wood chinking and clay. Chimneys of crudely laid limestone (the brick is a recent replacement) provided for fireplaces upstairs and down. The interior seems very spacious, for the rooms measure almost 20 by 20 feet each, and the ceilings vary in height from eight feet in the front rooms to nine feet in the extension. Logs and filling were left uncovered inside, and marks of axe and adz are very obvious, as are shreds of the horsehair used for binding the clay. But there are paneled mantelpieces, and the exposed ceiling beams (expressed on the exterior) are chamfered along their edges. On some of them can been seen the

[27] Information from Misses Mary and Rebekah Peck.
[28] Information from Mrs. Selander, who thinks this house may originally have belonged to the Firestone family.

Roman numerals which marked their placement, and the wooden pegs holding them are also visible. The floors are of oak, and the original ceiling planks were of yellow poplar nailed with square-headed nails.

An equally fine house showing a different plan and elevation stands on the present Freeman property in Haymakertown.[29] This house, erected some time before 1783, also in a valley and near a spring, stands on a slope so that it has an exposed basement. The limestone walls of the basement are extended to form foundations for the log walls and for the large brick chimneys (the upper sections of these have recently been rebuilt). The present porch is not old, but there must have been some kind of porch or piazza giving access to the central front door. The house, 30 by 20 feet in size, is divided into two rooms on each floor by an off-center partition wall, against which is placed a narrow enclosed staircase. Only the first-floor rooms had fireplaces, for which large squared logs were used as lintels. These have recently been replaced by

[29] Mr. and Mrs. Freeman call this the Sessler house (a variant of the name Kesler), reporting a visit from descendants of a man born here in 1783.

3   Selander House: Mantelpiece

4   *Freeman House*

wood-paneled mantelpieces brought from a companion log dwelling on the property. The ceiling beams in the Freeman house are not merely chamfered, but are cut to form a half-round bead at the edges. The logs in the walls are somewhat larger than those in the Selander house and better fitted at the corners.

A similar plan was followed in the earliest section of the present Randolph house, which stands a few miles on the other side of Fincastle, on county route 640.[30] This may date back to the 1740's. The logs here, of exceptionally hard white oak, measure as much as 18 inches in section, as do some of the pine floor boards and paneling of the upper rooms. The adjoining section, built later, was put directly over the spring. Under one front corner of this extension, next to the chimney, there was a brick-lined pit for the storage of food. The ceiling beams in this extension have completely rounded corner beading.

One other variation in log buildings may be seen in the house on the property once owned by Colonel William Fleming, now the Monterey golf course on the edge of Roanoke.[31] Again the possum-trot plan was

[30] Information from Mrs. Ruth S. Randolph.   [31] Kegley, pp. 518–19.

5   *Freeman House: Detail of Log Construction*

used, but here the stairway to the attic rooms was built in the breeze-way, and the gable ends of the house were covered with weatherboards.

In addition to log houses, framed houses were also being erected by the pioneers as soon as sawn timber was available. Certainly by 1777 there was a sawmill in the Fincastle vicinity, for a court order of that year proposed to "establish a road from the court house to William Ward's sawmill,"[32] and another, Peter Shrader's, is mentioned in 1784.[33] This 1784 list names ten "frame dwelling houses," all having stone or brick chimneys. The houses of the Englishmen Thomas Bowyer and George Hancock are singled out: Bowyer's had four fireplaces and Hancock's three. The sole dwelling of brick mentioned was Jacob Carper's, and his was a "log, frame, and brick" combination. No doubt there was a mixing of framed timbers with logs in much of the building. When the Simmons house was dismantled in 1957, logs cut on only two sides were revealed in interior walls, under the lath and plaster. Attic

[32] Summers, p. 260.   [33] Stoner, p. 235.

6 *Log Kitchen*

rafters in one section were of pine poles with the bark left on. In cellars and attics of several Fincastle homes such bark-covered logs are still exposed.

Among the home owners credited with only a cabin in 1784 was Samuel McRoberts, who in 1792 built a home in the town on a plot opposite the present St. Mark's Church.[34] His log kitchen still stands, giving us a well-preserved example of the construction of such outbuildings—kitchens, smokehouses, granaries, barns. (Included in George Washington's list was a barn larger than any of the houses: 46 by 16 feet, "with stables on the broad side.") The logs in this Fincastle kitchen are smaller in diameter than those in the houses, and their ends project a bit more, but they are cut and fitted together in the same way.

During these early decades there were, of course, no architects. Civic buildings were planned by a few members of the governing board. In 1786, for example, Patrick Lockhart, Thomas Rowland, and George Hancock were in charge of planning the prison.[35] In 1793 John Miller, Henry Bowyer, and James Breckenridge laid out the clerk's office to be added to the courthouse.[36] Contractors for these buildings have already been mentioned, but there are no records of builders for any homes. Designated as carpenters or joiners were three immigrants among the Rangers of 1755: George Dars from Germany and Robert Hill and James McCoy from Ireland. Several of the Obenshains in Fincastle were carpenters, as were Henry and Adam Fizer. Benjamin Lanius is mentioned in 1808 as a carpenter, and John Woland and John Harsh as painters and plasterers. Samuel Cleage, an itinerant contractor who took pay in "gold, notes or negroes" as he traveled to Tennessee, may have done some building in Fincastle.[37] Carpenters and joiners may have assisted in the building of dwellings, but certainly many of them were put up by unskilled labor reinforced by neighborly cooperation. Dr. Doddridge praises the "native mechanical genius"—his father was one—"whose natural ingenuity enabled him to do many things for himself and his neighbors," who was "sufficiently the carpenter to build the best kind of houses then in use, that is to say, first a cabin, and afterwards the hewed log-house, with a shingled roof."[38]

But there were, even early, more elaborate dwellings than those we have been considering. To see a good example of one we must travel the

---

[34] According to residents of the area.   [35] Summers, p. 414.   [36] *Ibid.*, p. 454.
[37] Stoner, pp. 37–38, 209. Cleage (Clelage or Cleagles) had left Botetourt County in 1823.   [38] Kercheval, pp. 276–77.

short distance of a mile and a half northwest of Fincastle to the present Slusser property beyond the old fairgrounds. Here a fine farmhouse was built, perhaps in the 1740's, on part of Benjamin Borden's great land grant. [39] Its owner remains unknown, but townspeople suggest that he was either Major William Trigg or Benjamin Borden himself.

This clapboard-covered log house, known locally as Promised Land, is still occupied and has undergone little change since it was built. It illustrates for us the Valley of Virginia style which continued to be popular for over a century. In plan it is simple, having a wide central hall on each of its two floors, with one room opening off either side of the halls. But on the front is a double-storied porch with solid walnut columns, and the entrance door is framed with rectangular overhead and side lights. Chimneys at each end provide fireplaces for every room, and the tall windows (6 feet high and 3½ feet wide) rise almost to the ceilings. Interior walls are paneled, and the horizontal and vertical boards of some of the doors are arranged so as to form the double-cross pattern that supposedly repelled evil spirits and occasioned the popular name of "witch door." Locks and hardware were imported from England. Although crooked walls and ceilings indicate the crude construction techniques, Promised Land still has so much charm that we can easily imagine its fine appearance two centuries ago.

These, then, were the types of dwellings. Let us look now at some of the streets, homes, and businesses in Fincastle, largely as defined for us in policies taken out by Fincastle householders with the new Mutual Assurance Society Against Fire on Buildings of the State of Virginia, started in Richmond in 1795. [40]

On September 29, 1798, Stephen Trigg took out a policy to cover his dwelling house which was valued at $2,200, his kitchen at $500, and his lumber house at $250. The house was 51 feet in front and 18 feet deep, built of wood, and there was a wing measuring 16½ by 16½ feet. The first story of the house was used as "a retail store of dry goods and hard wares." His lumber house measured 20 by 29 feet, and the kitchen, set back 18 feet from the house for safety, was even larger: 36 by 19½ feet. Both were built of wood and both had two stories. The Trigg house stood on "Round Oak" (Roanoke) Street between "the house of James

[39] Stoner, pp. 273–74.

[40] Mutual Assurance policies discussed in the following paragraphs are numbered as follows: Trigg, No. 30; Mary Trigg, No. 886; Harvey, Nos. 29 and 884; Wilson, No. 2299; Navil, Nos. 56 and 851; Rudisill, No. 250; Griffin, No. 240; and Kyle, No. 244.

Matt. Early and John Gofford"; the Early lot was on the southwest corner of Main and Roanoke Streets.

Also on Roanoke Street, on the corner of Main Street facing the courthouse, stood the wooden, two-storied dwelling of Matthew Harvey. His policy, also dated September 29, 1798, insured his house for $3,500. But his lumber house, and his kitchen, built of stone, were not insured. Two establishments on Main Street were insured a few years later: in 1804 Alexander Wilson's store and dwelling for $1,800 and in 1805 John Navil's dwelling for $1,100 and his kitchen for $100. In 1811 Jacob Rudisill insured his dwelling on Church Street for $2,000 and his combined kitchen and workshop for $700.

In March of 1811 John C. Griffin and William and David Kyle took out policies which enable us to visualize Main Street two blocks down from the courthouse corner, for drawings on their policies show buildings adjoining their property. Along the 33-foot-wide street there were log and frame buildings, some with one story and some with two. Some buildings had shingled roofs. There was one small building of stone, and also a market house with stone pillars, which stood on the corner of Water Street, a block from the town spring.

John Griffin's house, like Matthew Harvey's a two-storied frame building, was insured for $3,350. To this was added insurance for his store, at $900, his kitchen, at $250, his granary, at $140, and his smokehouse, at $40.

On the southwest corner of Main and Water Streets stood the group of six buildings insured by William and David Kyle. The dwelling, which faced the stone-pillared market house, was again two-storied with a shingled roof and measured 34 feet across the front by 24 feet in depth. This home, insured in 1811 for $1,800, must be the present Crowder house, for the location and the dimensions correspond exactly. A record of the prison bounds set in 1810 mentions "Kyle's New House" on this very place, too, and years later the Kyle estate was receiving rent for what is now the Crowder home.[41] Originally the house had no front porch; the door opened directly on the street, as the sketch on the insurance policy indicates. The walls are of log covered by weatherboards, and the rooms flanking the hall still have their original floor boards and some old windowpanes. Attic windows still have handmade blinds put together with wooden pegs.

Fifty-one feet away from the house were the adjoining counting-

[41] Stoner, p. 425.

house and storehouse of the Kyles, these being set back from Main Street to allow for a 3-foot-wide porch along their entire 70-foot length. The countinghouse was built of logs, 16½ by 40½ feet in size, and the storehouse of frame, 20 by 30 feet. Both were two stories high, and each was valued at $1,400. Behind stood a separate one-story kitchen, a granary, and a large 20-by-24-foot stable, facing Water Street.

The most elaborate and costly houses of the decades between 1770 and 1820 were built, not in the village itself, but on the little hills nearby. They were sturdily constructed of brick, stone, or finely finished wood, well proportioned and tastefully decorated. Available to owners, carpenters, and masons were many architectural handbooks from which could be taken plans, sections, and details of decoration; with care and taste, even in an area still a near-wilderness, it was possible to have a fine home.

One of these was the home of Mary Harvey Trigg, Stephen Trigg's wife, built near Promised Land. Her father, Robert Harvey, had begun

8   *Hawthorne Hall*

the house shortly after her marriage in 1795, and it was finished by 1801. Presumably her husband's combined house and retail store in Fincastle was not fine enough for her. When in 1804 (after her husband's departure on a long journey which left her widowed) she had these buildings revalued and reinsured, Samuel Wilson was occupying the property and using it as a place for his tavern.[42] But the new house, now known as Hawthorne Hall and still used by the Slusser family, is very handsome indeed. Its walls are of Flemish-bonded brick, 14 inches thick, and it is one-and-a-half stories high, with strongly accented end chimneys. In addition to the kitchen in the basement there was a separate kitchen on the left-hand side, which was originally

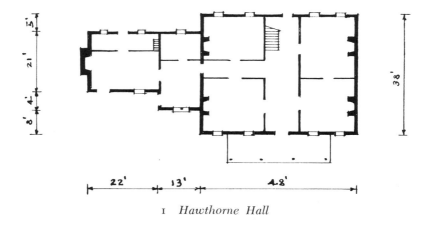

1   *Hawthorne Hall*

connected to the house by an open breezeway. On either side of the central hall are two large, high-ceilinged rooms, with smaller rooms in the attic. Across the front there ran originally a columned porch with a central arched opening. This matched the arched overhead light of the main entrance, and the curve is repeated in the lovely elliptical arch spanning the central hall. The rooms are ornamented with vertically fluted molding, slender columns, and finely paneled walls. The delicacy of the details and in particular the fine Adam décor of the drawing-room mantelpiece, flanked by arched niches in which once hung full-length mirrors, show the new taste which was supplanting the older Georgian—the Federal style of the early Republic.

[42] *Ibid.*, p. 420–21, and insurance policy No. 886.

9   *Hawthorne Hall: Mantelpiece*

Best example of this style, larger and more elaborate, was the brick mansion built by General James Breckenridge, which was called Grove Hill. It crowned a knoll on his magnificent estate in the Catawba Creek area, two miles northwest of Fincastle and not far from Hawthorne Hall. Grove Hill was destroyed by fire in 1909,[43] and only one small brick outbuilding and a few traces of the mansion's foundations remain. Comments by those Fincastle residents who remember it from half a century ago match the sentiment expressed by John Edwards Caldwell in 1808: in a letter referring to General Breckenridge he remarks that "his house is elegant and his demesne handsomely laid out."[44] We assume that Grove Hill was newly built when General Breckenridge insured it in 1804, for surely he would have done so earlier had the house been finished. He knew about the insurance; his signature appears on the policies of Matthew Harvey and Stephen Trigg. His own policy puts the impressive valuation of $10,000 on the house and $2,000 on the attached kitchen.[45] (This, for the kitchen, was $200 more than for the Kyle home.)

[43] Information from Mr. Raymond P. Barnes.   [44] Stoner, p. 154.
[45] Mutual Assurance policies Nos. 1137, 2319, and 2320.

10 *Grove Hill*

Obviously General and Mrs. Breckenridge were aware of current architectural fashion, for the mansion was a lovely example of the Federal style. Its Flemish-bonded brick walls rose two and one-half stories above stone foundations, and there were white wooden porches, reached by sandstone steps, on the front and on the sides. Over the entrance door was a typical Federal fanlight, echoed by the arch of the Palladian window above and the curved window in the pediment. According to the insurance policy, this "elegantly finished" dwelling measured 50 by 60 feet, with a "Sellar the whole size of the house." Within, there were two large halls crossing at right angles, and, Fincastle residents say, twenty-six rooms, all except four in the attic heated by fireplaces. Old photographs show the four large chimneys, as well as the fine window trim, horizontal banding, and cornices of the exterior. And townspeople still speak of the elaborately carved mantelpieces, moldings, and staircases. Attached to the main building was a two-story kitchen, also of brick, measuring 21 by 47 feet "with an open Piaser at one side." A brick smokehouse, an office, and a wooden stable stood at the rear of the mansion, the stable alone being insured for $100.

11 *Santillane*

In 1804 General Breckenridge paid personal property tax on 24 horses, as well as on 49 slaves.[46]

Another impressive brick mansion, probably built a few years earlier than Grove Hill and still occupied, is Santillane, which stands on a little rise just southwest of the town of Fincastle. Its builder and first owner was probably Colonel George Hancock; a letter written by his daughter Peggy in 1805 is headed "Santillane, Botetourt."[47] It was Hancock's

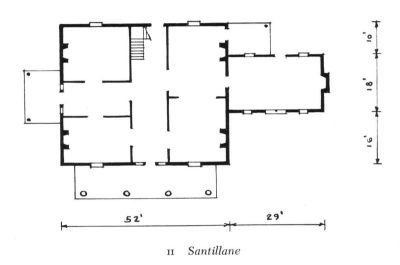

II   *Santillane*

younger daughter, Judy, however, who had caught the attention of William Clark when he rescued her from a balky horse, and it was she for whom he named Judith River in Montana. After returning from his westward expedition he went to Fincastle to court and marry Judy, and the citizens of the town took the opportunity to congratulate him with an "address." Clark's partner, Meriwether Lewis, did not fare so well in Fincastle. Miss Letitia Breckenridge departed for Richmond when rumors spread that he was planning to court her.[48]

Santillane, now owned by Mr. and Mrs. Robert Stoner, is similar in

[46] Botetourt County Personal Property Tax Lists, 1804 (filed in Virginia State Library, Richmond).

[47] Stoner, p. 407, and information from Mr. Stoner, who has a photostated copy of the letter.

[48] John Bakeless, *Lewis and Clark, Partners in Discovery* (New York, 1947), pp. 114–15, 195, 381–85.

structure to Grove Hill but more Georgian in effect. It retained the
Valley of Virginia double-storied front porch (later replaced by a
columned portico) and there were smaller porches to side entrances.
On the east is the interesting detail of Santillane's four false windows:
what appear to be closed shutters are placed over the fireplaces on this

12   Santillane: Hallway

side of the house. Perhaps they were used for practical reasons, to save on the cost of construction or of heating the house, or perhaps to copy similar sham windows used in eastern Virginia to avoid the taxes placed there on true ones. But since this is the side of the house approached from the road their primary value lies in enhancement of the architectural design. On the interior of Santillane two drawing rooms, a dining room, and a library flank the wide central hall on the first floor, and a second-floor hall and bedrooms are arranged in similar fashion. This upper hall, wide enough to serve as a living room, originally opened on the second story of the entrance porch. All the rooms in Santillane are marked by their beautiful, spacious proportions and by the restrained elegance of their woodwork and mantelpieces. To the west of the mansion stood the kitchen, and behind were smokehouse, slave quarters, and other outbuildings. The exceptionally flat area of the grounds in front of the house bears witness to the truth of the tradition that the top of the hill had been leveled off by slave labor.

About five miles south of Fincastle, west of the present route 220, stood two important estates.[49] One was Greenfield, owned by Colonel William Preston. Since the 1740's a small log structure here had served as both fort and house, and this, with the land, was purchased by Colonel Preston in 1761 from Stephen Rentfroe. Preston enlarged the building, and later, about 1840, a new wing was added at right angles to the older section. Until Greenfield was unfortunately destroyed by fire in 1959, it was a notable landmark in this area of the state. Fairly near the site of Greenfield, however, still stands Holladay Place, built about 1810 for a granddaughter of Colonel Preston by her mother, on the occasion of her marriage to Lewis Holladay. This brick dwelling is again of the Federal or Early Republican style, with handsome square posts on the large front porch, door framed with lights, and fine carpenter locks. The frame wing at the rear was added in mid-nineteenth-century manner, to provide kitchen and dining room.

In addition to brick mansions there were several in the county built of stone. One of these was the home now known as Stonelea, originally belonging to a Methodist minister, Edward Mitchell, and visited more than once by Bishop Asbury. Mitchell had bought, in 1799, a section of land including a hill with a large spring at its foot, six miles south of Fincastle and about a mile distant from Greenfield. On Mitchell's site were the foundations of the earlier house of David Cloyd, notable as the

---

[49] Kegley, p. 321 (photograph), pp. 506–7; Stoner, pp. 93–94, 313.

13   *Stonelea: Site*

site of an Indian attack in 1764. The basement of the extant house, with
its earthen floor, log ceiling, and high fireplace, is perhaps the kitchen of
Cloyd's wooden dwelling.[50]

Mitchell undoubtedly knew the stone houses of Pennsylvania, a type
which new settlers were introducing to the Valley, and he was lucky
enough to have on his hill an abundance of the soft gray limestone
which was commonly used for buildings in the Quaker State.[51] One can
see the outcroppings of this colorful bluish or yellowish gray rock on the
front lawn and the large pit on the side created by the excavators.
According to local tradition, Mitchell hired for the quarrying and
building some Italian stonemasons who had been brought to this

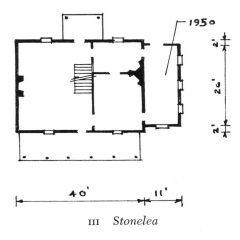

III   *Stonelea*

country by George Washington to build canals, paying them ten cents a
day plus room and board. They did their work well, for Mitchell's house
and barn, now belonging to the Weeks estate, are in almost perfect condition.

Stonelea was presumably built soon after Mitchell bought the property. It is a durable house, 40 feet wide by 28 feet deep, with heavy
walls 29 inches thick at the base and 22 inches thick in the upper walls.
The weight of the cornerstones has been estimated to be between five
and seven hundred pounds. The stone, laid irregularly in the side and
rear walls, is more carefully cut and set in regular courses on the front,
with simulated arches over widow openings. Stonelea varies from the

[50] Kegley, pp. 501–3; Stoner, pp. 434–36. Information about the house and property
comes from the late Mrs. Howard Weeks.
[51] For comparative Pennsylvania houses, see Stotz, pp. 46–49, 98, and for barn, p. 146.

14   *Stonelea*

usual Virginia pattern in that it has no central hallway: from the front porch two doors lead directly into first-floor rooms. On the left was originally the master bedroom, and on the right were a dining room and kitchen with fireplaces which opened from a single triangular chimney. There were two narrow winding staircases at the back, which were used by boys and girls in the family to reach their segregated sleeping quarters on the second floor. The youngest child slept in a "keeping room" off the master bedroom. The original fireplaces were of lime-stone, with yellow poplar mantelpieces, and the inner walls were finished with lime plaster applied directly to the stone.

To the east of Stonelea was attached a two-story wooden extension, the lower room used for gathering goose down for mattresses and the upper room for looming. A wing behind the house, built of logs but embellished with Germantown hooded porches, held the kitchen and servants' rooms. (Mitchell did not have the slaves which Breckenridge had. He had freed his in 1790, and in 1804 he paid personal property tax on only four white servants.[52]) There is evidence of other log

[52] Botetourt County Personal Property Tax Lists, 1804; see Stoner, p. 368, on manumission.

outbuildings and of an outdoor oven used for baking bread. A water-wheel-and-bucket system devised by Mitchell brought water from the spring at the foot of the hill up to the house. Next to the spring he built a stone and wood bank barn like those so often seen in Pennsylvania and here in the Valley, both to keep the cattle warm and to allow wagons to drive directly up to the second story from the back.

Facing Santillane from a higher hill to the east, from which it commands a spectacular view of Fincastle and the Valley, stands the mansion called Prospect, now owned by Mrs. James McDowell. It was built perhaps as early as 1819 by John Gray, and because of its windy site was then called Gray's Folly.[53] This again is Federal in style and follows the usual Valley of Virginia style, here somewhat more refined than in the earlier examples. Prospect is built of wood, with a smooth surface of flush boarding, and trimmed with a fine beaded molding. The more delicate scale of the present porch suggests that this is of

[53] Information from manuscript by Neville McDowell (January, 1951), filed in Roanoke Public Library, and from Stoner, p. 430.

15   *Prospect*

16   *Prospect: Hall Stairway*

later-nineteenth-century date, and the two side wings were added in the 1940's. But the original details too are delicate and charming: the oval overhead lights of the doors, the Adam sunbursts on the mantels, the vertically fluted moldings, the carved trim on the staircase, and the stenciled patterns on the base paneling of the walls.

There were as yet in the village of Fincastle itself no such mansions, although there were a few costly houses like Matthew Harvey's. But there was growing activity within the town.

From the beginning there were taverns. Part of the business transacted by the justices during those first meetings in the spring of 1770 was to grant licenses for ordinaries: to Stephen Trigg in April, to James McGavock and James McDowell in May.[54] Within a few months there were five or six ordinaries at Botetourt Courthouse, and their number increased through the decades. The court had also fixed rates for these establishments: "For French brandy 5 shillings per gallon . . . for a warm diet with small Beer nine pence . . . for lodging in clean sheets, one in a bed, six pence; if two in a bed, three pence three farthings; if more than two, nothing."[55]

Especially from the 1780's on, Fincastle attracted many skilled craftsmen and businessmen, and the court kept on issuing merchants' licenses in growing numbers: twenty-two individuals obtained licenses to retail goods between 1787 and 1789.[56] A typical advertisement was that for Daniel Houry's Hatting Business in 1800:

He has always on hand all kinds of Hats both the ancient and newest fashions, which he will sell on the most reasonable terms, either for Cash, good fur, wool, or such produce as may suit him. The highest price is given for fur & good wool.[57]

Agricultural and stockraising activity of course continued. And the space devoted by a newspaper of 1801 to a lengthy essay on a method of preventing the premature decay of peach trees shows the early interest in the development of the large fruit orchards still so typical of this section of western Virginia.[58] (The appraisal made for George Washington in 1775 has attached this statement: "N. B. There is near 2000 peach stones cornols planted on said tract of land.")

Since March of 1800 Fincastle had published a weekly newspaper, priced at 15 shillings or two dollars a year. This was the *Herald of*

[54] Summers, pp. 74, 81.   [55] *Ibid.*, pp. 64–65.   [56] Kegley, pp. 410–11.
[57] *Herald of Virginia*, December 5, 1800.
[58] *Fincastle Weekly Advertiser*, May 8, 1801.

Virginia and Fincastle Weekly Advertiser, which in 1801 dropped the first half of its title. In 1820 the newspaper became the *Herald of the Valley.*[59] There were also in the town three schools: the Botetourt Seminary, which was chartered in 1785, the Reverend Robert Logan's Classical School, which opened in 1800, and, sometime after 1796, a public school.[60]

By the early 1800's, too, there was need for new churches. In 1771 an acre of land had been set aside for an Episcopal church, but it is not known exactly when it was built or what it looked like. We can visit the site and see the graveyard, where some unmarked stones probably are older than the earliest inscribed ones of 1795 and 1797. Certainly the church existed in 1785, for it was closed in that year (when the Act for Establishing Religious Freedom was passed) and not reopened until about 1795, when the Presbyterians took it over.[61]

Francis Asbury had preached to the Methodists of Fincastle on May 24, 1794, and several times thereafter, but the congregation did not then have a church, and the meetings were held in private dwellings. On September 5, 1802, Asbury recorded in his *Journal* that his meeting "continued four hours, and there was a moving among the people. I lodged at Edward Mitchell's. I drew a plan of a house 40 feet long, 30 feet wide, and 2 stories high, of brick—to be built in Fincastle; two-thirds of the money must be collected before we begin. This, like many more of my good designs, may come to naught."[62] In 1803 a half-acre of land was conveyed to the trustees of the Methodist congregation by Patrick Lockhart and his wife (in consideration of twelve pounds) for a church to be built three blocks south of the Episcopal-Presbyterian site.[63] Unfortunately there is no record of it except for the fact that it was built of brick, because it was replaced by the present church in 1840. So, although site and graveyard survive, it is not known whether Asbury's good design materialized.

In 1813 the Presbyterians petitioned to be given permission to build a new church, saying that the old one they had inherited from the Episcopalians was "in so decayed and ruinous condition as to render it

[59] Stoner, pp. 255–56.

[60] Irwin B. Cohen and others, *An Economic and Social Survey of Botetourt County* (University of Virginia, School of Rural Social Economics; Charlottesville, Va., 1942), p. 129; Stoner, p. 485.

[61] The Rev. J. M. Holladay, *A Partial History of Fincastle Presbyterian Church* (Richmond, Va., 1902), pp. 12–13, 28.

[62] Stoner, p. 371.   [63] *Ibid.,* pp. 372–73.

no longer fit for use."[64] But it was not until 1818 that the new one was erected. This was Georgian in style, square in plan with a hipped roof topped by a belfry, as we can see in an engraving for which the sketches were done in 1843.[65] Its entrance faced east toward the old spring and market area, and on the west was an attached low wing for the session house. Parts of the brick walls of this church remain in the present structure, and some marks of its windows may still be seen.

A new courthouse, too, was built between 1818 and 1820, after drawings made by Thomas Jefferson.[66] A letter written from Monticello

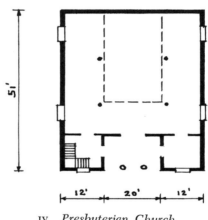

IV   *Presbyterian Church*

on October 6, 1818, to General James Breckenridge mentions that the drawings are on the way, "with the explanations accompanying them," and adds, "I hope your workmen will sufficiently understand them." Nothing remains of this structure, and the only sketch recording it is a very crude little one on a map of 1832, which shows a domed central unit flanked by one-story offices. We know it had a portico, for this is mentioned in records of payments to William Barton, the contractor, and his helpers. The whole community shared in this enterprise. John Peck supplied the walnut logs for the columns of the portico. The logs were hauled by James Walker and Thomas Bennett, turned by Frederick Boseman and Mr. Douthat, bored by C. Harshbarger. Poplar planks for

[64] *Ibid.*, pp. 238–39.
[65] Reproduced on the title page of this book, from Henry Howe, *Historical Collections of Virginia* (Charleston, S.C., 1847), p. 202. For description, see Holladay, pp. 18–19.
[66] See Stoner, pp. 179–82, for all documentary information on this courthouse.

covering and ceiling of the portico were furnished by H. Walker (at $11.50 for 900 feet), and R. and H. Kyle supplied "carving and ceiling portico and landing." Stone flooring was provided by Nathaniel Minor, shingles were made by H. Wax, W. Cook, and John Waggoner, and the plastering was done by D. T. White. Other citizens did copper and tin work, painting, or "blowing rock" and supplied the needed fittings.

There had also been built a newer jail, two stories high, with seven apartments, each with its own fireplace. But according to a report filed on September 5, 1823, although the debtors' apartment was fine, large, and airy, the others, for criminals, were too small and too few.[67]

By 1822 the town of Fincastle had reached its half-century mark, and it was neatly defined in a map drawn by surveyor John Wood. This shows 103 lots, carefully numbered and apportioned to 67 owners. There were as yet only 63 taxable buildings, but construction and business were to show a sharp rise in the coming decades. The town was becoming self-sufficient and self-conscious: in 1823 the *Herald of the Valley* was succeeded by the *Fincastle Mirror*.

The formative period had definitely drawn to a close by 1822. Later periods were to leave their mark on the appearance of the town, but the basic pattern of street width and placement, of courthouse and church locations, of lots for home ownership, of types of buildings, had been set. The first stage had passed, but fortunately for us, many souvenirs of it remain.

[67] *Ibid.*, pp. 190–91.

ANTEBELLUM FINCASTLE

II

THE visitor to Fincastle today can easily use as a guide the map made by John Wood in 1822. The streets follow the same pattern and bear the same names, and the major landmarks—spring, courthouse, and churches—are still there. In fact, once located within the confines of the map, the visitor seems at home in the small peaceful town of the 1820's, its appearance almost unchanged by twentieth-century intrusions. But the very neatness of the town today, matching the neatness of the map, may mislead him. He may forget that then the streets were unpaved and dusty, that most of the houses now so primly white and clap-boarded then revealed their homely construction, that most of the 103 lots so precisely numbered and apportioned to their owners by Mr. Wood were still undeveloped, and that the slopes of the gentle Virginia hills framing the settlement were still untamed.

But more and more settlers were coming to build their homes in Fincastle and to set up shops or trades in the rapidly growing county seat. In 1825 there were only 63 taxable buildings. Of these, 47 were valued under $1,000. Ten were valued between $1,000 and $2,500, and only six appear in the over-$2,500 category. Two of these, at $2,600 each, were the establishments (not the single dwellings) of John C. Griffin and Jacob Rudisill. Henry Bowyer's property is valued at $2,850,

Robert Kyle's at $3,600, and John Moore's and Matthew Harvey's at $3,700 each.[1] In 1835, however, when Joseph Martin published his *New and Comprehensive Gazetteer of Virginia,* he could say that Fincastle was a "flourishing and wealthy village" with 260 homes and 3 churches. There were then, all told, 703 inhabitants: 468 white, 192 slave, 43 free colored.[2] (Fincastle in the census of 1960 had 403 inhabitants.)

Businesses mentioned by Joseph Martin included six "mercantile stores," two clock- and watch-makers, two druggist shops, and three taverns. One tavern was run by William Craft near the courthouse on the corner of Back Street and Roanoke Street. It was the old Union Hotel which he had bought in September, 1824, from Ruth Nece, who had tried running it for a few months after her father's death in March.[3] Another was operated by Mrs. Backus in the Kyle house on the corner of Main and Water Streets.[4] The third was perhaps that run by Edward Dennis in Stephen Trigg's house on Roanoke Street, for Dennis was its proprietor in 1820.[5] Or it may have been Rudisell's tavern, advertised in 1824.[6] One of the "mercantile stores" was that run by the Kyles. Perhaps already established were those advertising in newspapers of the 1840's: the goods store of Utz and Hannah, the "Dutch Store" of S. Springer and Company, the dry-goods store of Shanks and Anderson: "New York and Philadelphia at Your Door!"[7] Samuel C. Whiteside, silver-smith and jeweler, had a shop on Main Street, and T. G. Godwin sold clocks.[8]

Then Joseph Martin lists the services offered by four boot and shoe factories, four saddlers, two tailors, and two hatters. One of the boot and shoe factories was James H. Bickle's, which opened in June of 1824; another, W. H. Nelson's, opened two months later, on Main Street.[9] Jacob Carper's saddler's shop was running by 1823, "on the Main Street three doors above the store of R. and H. Kyle and opposite the house of Dr. McDowell." He sold "Real Spanish Saddles" at prices ranging from $18 to $35 (plain ones ran $8 to $20), reminding his clientele that "every Saddle with a *Horn to it* IS NOT A SPANISH ONE." Carper, like most of the merchants, was willing to take country produce in lieu of cash.[10]

[1] Tax Lists for Fincastle, 1825 (filed in Virginia State Library).
[2] Charlottesville, Va., 1835, p. 328.
[3] *Fincastle Mirror,* September 5, 1823; March 12, June 23, September 24, 1824.
[4] Robert D. Stoner, *A Seed-Bed of the Republic* (Roanoke, Va., 1962), pp. 170, 425.
[5] *Ibid.,* p. 170.   [6] *Mirror,* June 18, 1824.
[7] *Fincastle Democrat,* May 18, June 20, 1846.
[8] *Ibid.,* June 20, 1846; December 8, 1845.   [9] *Mirror,* June 4, August 13, 1824.
[10] *Ibid.,* August 29, 1823; *Democrat,* May 18, 1846.

A new saddle and harness-making shop was set up by Charles F. Anderson and George W. Tizzard in 1850.[11] Among the tailors of the 1820's was Henry A. Skaggs, whose business was next to Carper's saddler's shop.[12] Tailors of the 1840's included Michael McCarthy, Baker and Hollandy, and James C. Hazelwood.[13] When Hazelwood was appointed jailer of Botetourt County, he was required to reside in the jail; so he set up shop "in the basement room at the south end," offering "TAILORING! Cheaper than Ever!"[14]

Other establishments listed by Joseph Martin were those of five cabinetmakers and house joiners, a coppersmith and tin-plate worker, four blacksmiths, and four wagonmakers. Then there were also two tanners, two wheelwrights, a gunsmith, and a chairmaker. One of the blacksmith shops, in the little brick building on Main Street across from the present-day jail, was run, according to townspeople, by Billy Smith. This shop has been doubled in size by its present owner, Erne LaBell, but the original western section still exhibits its sturdy walls of brick laid three deep, its hand-hewn roof beams, and its old door with a large, 16-inch, handmade hinge. Also mentioned as blacksmiths of these decades are James T. Robinson and James Doud.[15] The brick chair factory on Murray Street, now enlarged and changed, had on its first floor machinery connected by pulleys through openings in the floor to a basement workshop. (In later years this building was used as a dress-maker's and tailor's shop by the Hedrick family, which still owns it.) In the yard of Mr. Carper Hedrick's house opposite the Methodist Church are foundations of a wheelwright's shop.[16] Fincastle, by Martin's listing, had an oil mill, also a flour mill with a wool-carding machine: this was Benjamin Ammen's on Miller's Creek, long to be known for its excellent blankets.[17]

Joseph Martin mentions, too, a confectionary and "a printing office issuing a weekly newspaper," which in his day was the *Fincastle Democrat*. The *Fincastle Mirror* had in 1829 been supplanted by the *Virginia Patriot*, which ran until 1834. It then gave way to the *Democrat*, which was issued on into the 1850's.[18] There were nine attorneys in the town (among those mentioned or placing notices in the newspapers

[11] *Democrat*, December 21, 1850.   [12] *Mirror*, October 27, 1823; October 21, 1828.
[13] *Democrat*, December 8, 1845.   [14] *Ibid.*, May 18, 1846.
[15] *Ibid.*, March 27, 1847.
[16] Information about the chair factory and the wheelwright's shop from Mr. Carper Hedrick.
[17] Stoner, p. 410.   [18] *Ibid.*, pp. 256–57.

of these decades were Hugh Meenan and a Mr. Woodville in 1823, and John Wilson, John W. Jones, George W. Wilson, John T. Anderson, and Joseph R. Glasgow in 1845).[19] And there were three regular physicians, a temperance society, and a "well-organized" fire department.

The *Gazetteer* speaks of three churches, Presbyterian, Methodist, and Episcopal, of which we shall say more later, and of one male and one female academy. To just which schools Joseph Martin was referring is not clear, for there were several for which we find notices during this general period. Perhaps the Fincastle Female Academy was already functioning in the 1830's. An announcement made by its principal, Mrs. L. Bonnelle, in 1846, calls it the "Fincastle English and French Female Academy," but French was extra ($8), as were "Drawing, Painting, and various kinds of needlework" (also $8).[20] The Fincastle Female Seminary was not incorporated until 1849.[21]

Then there was a Fincastle Academy which offered college preparation for both sexes. It had opened in October of 1823, according to the published announcement by Enoch Sullivan, Israel Hamilton, and George P. Digges. A student enrolled in this academy could follow a curriculum of "Spelling, Reading, Writing, and Arithmetic" for $12 per annum and add "Latin, Greek, and Mathematics" for $24 more. Study of "Geography and the Use of Globes" added $10 to the fee, but it cost $20 to be trained in "Rhetoric, Logic, Moral Philosophy, English Composition, Natural and Universal History or either." The advertisement stated that "all possible exertions will be employed by the teachers for the comfort and advancement of the pupils committed to their care" and that "young Gentlemen" would be "fitted to enter the most respectable colleges." The summer vacation in 1824 ran from July 30 to August 30, and for its second session the school fixed a comprehensive rate for board and tuition of $85 a year.[22]

A school of classics and sciences, the old Botetourt Seminary revived, was begun in 1836 in an octagonal building at first shared with the Free Masons, who had built it (they met on the second floor). This was first taught by an English Presbyterian, the Reverend Thomas Brown, and had almost a hundred boys enrolled, many of them being boarders from the southwestern area of Virginia. Tuition and board here, in 1838, amounted to $120 or $130. Most expensive subjects, judging from the

[19] *Herald of the Valley*, January 4, 1823; *Democrat*, December 8, 1845.
[20] *Democrat*, October 3, 1846.   [21] Stoner, p. 481.
[22] *Mirror*, October 31, 1823; July 30, 1824.

notice published by J. L. Gillespie, A.M., principal in 1846, were "Ancient Languages or Mathematics, $30." French or Spanish were extra, at $12. This school stood on the hill where is now the Negro church, and when it was torn down its bricks were re-used to lay Fincastle sidewalks.[23]

Worthy of mention, too, are the Fincastle Library, moved by its president John C. Griffin to the *Mirror* office in 1823, and H. G. Gaines's scrivener's office, in which deeds, contracts, or other documents were drawn up for anyone who applied.[24]

Then there was entertainment. Some was provided by local talent: the Botetourt Springs Thespians gave a play on Christmas Eve in 1824, at 6:30 P.M., for fifty cents.[25] Some was imported and exotic, like the "GRAND MANAGERIE [*sic*] of LIVING VARMINTS" exhibited in June of 1846 by Brimstone and Cataract: "The Nantucket Sea-Serpent . . . the indescribable Yu-rang-yu-tang (who drinks 3 gallons of hard cider per hour) . . . the great Elephant Tip-Toe Sultan (he will carry a barrel of cider on his tusks, and suffer a large batch of pancakes to be fried upon his ears)." Following on this, in October, Welch, Mann & Delavan's Great National Circus brought its "Great Equestrian Cavalcade"—150 men and horses—with a brass band with thirteen musicians "in an elegant and costly chariot drawn by 12 beautiful cream colored horses." They set up at Fincastle their "great waterproof pavillion tent, superbly finished . . . 20,000 square feet in its dimensions" which could "with ease contain 3000 persons." Tickets to either of these attractions, too, cost only fifty cents, with "children and colored servants half-price."[26]

All this varied activity reflected expansion and change in the town. Plans were made for new homes, new churches, a new courthouse, and into the conservative colonial and Federal patterns of Fincastle's architecture began to filter elements from the Classic and Gothic Revival styles becoming so popular throughout the country.

But they came slowly. Most of Fincastle's families continued to build simple clapboarded log and frame houses of traditional plan and neat trim, like the small Hammitt (now Kessler) house on the southeast corner of Main and Water Streets, where the kitchen was once a separate structure. The Simmons house, destroyed in 1957, which stood

[23] Rev. J. M. Holladay, *A Partial History of Fincastle Presbyterian Church* (Richmond, Va., 1902), pp. 45–46; Stoner, pp. 475–80; *Democrat*, October 3, 1846.

[24] *Mirror*, February 22, 1823; July 9, 1824.   [25] *Ibid.*, December 24, 1824.

[26] *Democrat*, June 20, October 3, 1846.

on the northeast corner of Main and Monroe Streets, was one of the larger and more handsome wooden buildings. When this house was dismantled, several earlier stages of the structure were revealed, showing progressive enlargements.[27] A heavy stone foundation enclosed an earthen-floored basement with large fireplace, and brick chimneys at both ends of the house provided for fireplaces for the other rooms. Evidently the western end of the house was the oldest, perhaps built before 1795, for the walls were of hewn logs and the rafters in the attic were pine poles, some still bark-covered. The framing of the eastern section, of the early nineteenth century, was of timber, and the attic rafters here were of sawn lumber. A remodeling which probably took place about 1840 was indicated by the more decorative fluting and beading of the mantelpieces placed in the eastern section, some fine paneled doors, and the distinctive treatment of stairs and hallway. Notable in the hallway were the panels of yellow poplar, 18 to 25 inches wide, and approximately 24 feet long, which reached from the cellar floor to the ceiling of the upstairs hall. The pegged staircase was so well constructed that in the dismantling of the house it was removed in one piece. The Simmons house in its final stage was an excellent example of the Valley of Virginia style, with its typical two-storied porch, above which rose a triangular pediment, and the rectangular overhead and side lights of its main entrance door.

There was in Fincastle an occasional house of brick, like the Thompson-Carper house on Roanoke Street opposite the present St. Mark's Church. Local residents say that this small house was probably built in the 1830's by Samuel Carruthers; the section of frame to the left and the kitchen wing at the back are of much later date. But now, within the town itself rather than on its outskirts, some residents were building fine brick homes with more stylish detail.

Notable for its taste and elegance is the dwelling built about 1826 by Benjamin Ammen on Catawba Street, close to his woolen mill.[28] The red brick walls of the Ammen house (now owned by Mrs. H. I. Switzer) have been painted white, and the lower section of the double-storied front porch, originally like the upper section, has been lengthened and changed. But the Adam style fan and side lights of the attractive entrance door remain. The central hall staircase is decorated with a

[27] Information from Mr. and Mrs. Harry Kessler, who made notes and photographs when the house was dismantled.
[28] Stoner, p. 410.

17   *Ammen House*

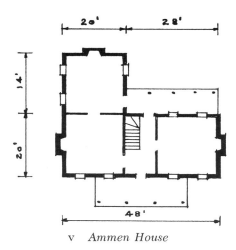

v   *Ammen House*

delicate scroll motif which was adapted from a design in one of the
newer handbooks: Owen Biddle's *The Young Carpenter's Assistant*,
published in Philadelphia in 1810 and sold there and in Richmond.[29]

[29] Plate 31. This plate was exactly copied in several houses in North Carolina, notably
by Jacob Stigerwalt. For these see F. B. Johnston and T. T. Waterman, *The Early
Architecture of North Carolina* (Chapel Hill, N.C., 1941), plates 214–17.

Mantels, doorframes, and chair rail are finely ornamented with a rope molding. All of this is still basically Federal in style, but again there is a note of the newer interests in the little pointed Gothic arches which appear in the upper frame of the doorway, and which are combined with classic column detail on the living-room mantelpiece.

Another of the finer homes was that of Robert Kyle. In 1820 Kyle bought from Jacob Lanius two lots in the center of Fincastle, at the crossing of Main and Church Streets and just west of the property of William and David Kyle with their wooden dwelling, countinghouse, and storehouse. On the Lanius lots stood a "mansion house and other buildings" which dated from before 1788, when they had been sold by Isaac Dawson to Lanius. But later deeds related to Robert Kyle's estate specifically mention a *brick* mansion, undoubtedly the handsome one still standing on the site, the present R. E. Bolton house and store.[30] In 1830 $1,300 was subtracted from the evaluation of two lots of Kyle's in Fincastle "for buildings removed" and in 1832 $5,000 was added for

[30] Information about deeds and the structure of the house from Mr. and Mrs. Roy Bolton, the present owners, who have restored it.

18   Ammen House: Stairway Design

buildings erected thereon.[31] This must have been for his new home.

We understand why so fine a house was built within the town when we note that the dwelling was combined with a dry-goods store. Residents of Fincastle still speak particularly of its stock of fine Irish linen, apparently now for the first time available in town. (The *Herald* of December 5, 1800, had carried an advertisement by Matthew Houston of "An Assortment of Goods" for sale at his house near the Natural Bridge, which included "casimeres, swandowns, Irish and German linens.")

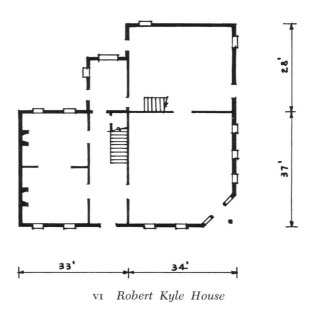

VI   *Robert Kyle House*

The Kyle house is of red brick on a gray limestone foundation, with windows and doors framed in sandstone, now painted white. Its walls are flush with the sidewalk so there are no porches, but the central section of a decorative wrought-iron balcony extending across the front has recently been re-erected. This is three spans in length; originally there were five spans. The entrance to the store, like that to the house, was on Main Street and was originally located at the point of the second window to the right of the house entrance. Its sandstone step was worn almost to the sidewalk and has been replaced. But the worn steps to the

[31] Botetourt County Land Tax Lists, 1830–1832 (filed in Virginia State Library, Richmond).

19   *Robert Kyle House: Stairway Detail*

hallway entrance remain, as do the grooves made in adjacent window ledges by customers sharpening their knives. The wide hallway which separates the store area from the dwelling continues through three stories and leads to spacious rooms on each floor. All of these are exuberantly decorated with woodwork carved, according to town tradition, by an itinerant German craftsman and show a delightful originality in the free treatment of traditional designs. Most of the motifs on hallway arches, staircases, mantelpieces, and wall recesses are "Pennsylvania Dutch": stars, tulips, leaves and vines, many-petaled flowers, and, notably in the front living-room mantelpiece, the type of pomegranate which bears a resemblance to thistle, pine cone, or pineapple. But there are other designs: Ionic scrolls and leaf-and-dart moldings, for example, which suggest that the carver was aware of the current Greek Revival style. His effects, however, are not at all architectural. They remain always suggestive of the butter molds, quilts, and carved chests of his folk-art background.

It was in the public buildings, however, that the new Revival styles took hold. The Episcopal congregation chose Gothic for their red brick

20   Robert Kyle House: Arch Flanking Fireplace

church, St. Mark's, on Roanoke Street. The original deed which may be seen in the church vestibule is dated August 16, 1837; the vestrymen, whose names are inscribed on a memorial plaque, paid $175 for the lot.[32]

St. Mark's is small, measuring only 35 by 46 feet in size, but it is one of the most charming buildings in Fincastle. The Gothic note here is quite restrained, for it appears only in the pointed arches and simply tracery of the entrance door and the windows. Otherwise the style is traditional Colonial in the steeple, the balconies, the hand-hewn pews. St. Mark's appears in the left foreground of Henry Howe's engraving, which shows also the Thompson-Carper house with the little eighteenth-century log kitchen behind it. To anyone who takes today the viewpoint chosen by the artist in 1843, it seems that Fincastle has changed not at all.

In 1840 the Methodist congregation built a new church.[33] Although this is not much larger than St. Mark's (44 by 56 feet; the extension in the rear was added in 1954), it has a different character because of its

[32] Stoner, p. 347.
[33] Eakin, Mrs. Harry R., *Historical Sketches of the Fincastle Methodist Church* (n.p., 1954), p. 28.

21   *St. Mark's Episcopal Church*

use of the Greek Revival style, stressed now in the architectural handbooks. One of the favorite books, Asher Benjamin's, was probably used by the builder of the Methodist Church. At any rate, he seems to have followed Benjamin's prescription that

a building erected for public worship should be so contrived as to produce in the beholder serious and devotional feelings. This effect is obtained by composing the building, generally, of large, bold, angular outlines, by continuing the entablature and cornices unbroken over the columns and pilasters, and giving all the decorations, either of moldings or sculpture, a large and grave appearance. . . . The windows should be large, and so constructed as to admit the air to circulate freely through the house, without producing a glare of light.[34]

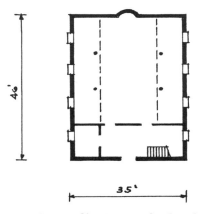

VII *St. Mark's Episcopal Church*

Such bold simple forms are to be seen in the Methodist façade, and we may note the tall shuttered windows. The Greek key patterns on upper frames of doors and windows are so close to one of Asher Benjamin's plates that they may well have followed it, and the moldings and panels of the entrance door appear to be freely adapted from several other plates.[35] Within the church ten Doric columns support a slave gallery which runs across the entrance wall and continues part of the way up the sides of the church. The entrance to this gallery is still called "the old slave door." The present steeple was built to replace the original small, square tower and spire after their destruction in a storm. Accord-

[34] *The Architect; or, Practical House Carpenter* (Boston, 1830), pp. 95–96.
[35] Plate 31, and cf. plates 22, 27, 28.

22 *St. Mark's Church and the Thompson-Carper House*

ing to a report written in 1882, the 126-pound bell in the tower had then been in use for forty years.[36] This would suggest that it had been acquired for the new church, although townspeople say it is dated 1811.

Rebuilding of the courthouse was begun in 1845, under the direction of the contractors Schuyler W. Smith and his partner Stratton, and was finished in 1848; the final report on its cost ($11,626.65) was made in

[36] *Fincastle Herald*, July 27, 1882.

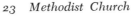

23   *Methodist Church*

May.[37] Town tradition is probably correct in its belief that Jefferson's design was used for this courthouse as well as for the earlier one, for certainly the general effect is Jeffersonian. Completely typical is the three-part arrangement of masses, with a prominent central section flanked by lower wings. Typical also is the use of pilasters and connected windows in these wings so as to give them a one-storied aspect,

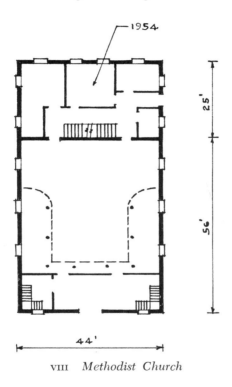

VIII   *Methodist Church*

although in reality they have two stories. But such forms appear also in the Greek Revival, and the courthouse, like the Methodist Church, uses

[37] Stoner, p. 183. The court records call the contractors simply Smith and Stratton, but townspeople affirm that the chief contractor was Schuyler W. Smith, who came from Bedford. According to a deed of October 3, 1872, filed in the Bedford courthouse, Schuyler W. Smith and his wife Hannah were then residents of Fincastle. There is an undocumented legend that Smith had worked on the buildings at Washington and Lee University and came from there to Fincastle for his first independent commission. He is not, however, included among the builders or contractors in the records kept by Washington and Lee (information from H. P. Scott, clerk of court, Bedford County, and E. S. Mattingly, treasurer, Washington and Lee).

24   *The Courthouse*

Greek details in its Doric columns, entablature, moldings, and pilasters. All have a rather heavy dignity, and all reflect the typical practice of translating classic forms into the language of American carpentry. The pilasters are more traditional than the rest, for they follow one of Asher Benjamin's plates imitated from the Choragic Monument of Thrasyllus, at Athens. In commenting on this, Benjamin noted that "its proportions are considered very beautiful when employed on works of no great

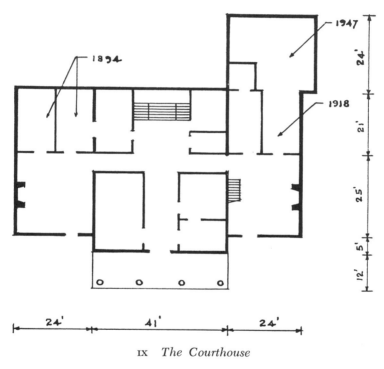

IX   *The Courthouse*

magnitude."[38] A steeple similar to those on the churches crowns the gabled roof, replacing the Jeffersonian dome. Funds for a town clock, which was purchased in Philadelphia for $350, were raised by public subscription.[39] The courthouse on completion provided a place for social functions: in 1849 the Aeolians, "a fine company of musical performers," gave there a concert of songs accompanied by violin, flute, and banjo.[40] The main body of the courthouse has remained un-

[38] Benjamin, plate 13, figure 2, and p. 37.
[39] *Democrat,* November 14, 1846; *Herald,* May 11, 1899.
[40] *Democrat,* April 21, 1849.

changed, but in 1894 a vault was added to preserve the county records,[41] and in 1918 and 1947 units for the clerk's office were built on the northeast corner.

The Presbyterians also chose the Greek Revival style when they enlarged their church in 1849,[42] and made the Greek note more emphatic still. They removed the session house and shifted the entrance of the church from east to south. Here they added a recessed porch and stair halls, and placed two Doric columns between flanking walls in the traditional Greek distyle-in-antis pattern. A new gabled roof and cornice of fairly satisfying classic proportions were added, and a new steeple was built. Again the result was the suitably "large and grave appearance" advocated by Asher Benjamin. The Presbyterian Church in its new dimensions of 44 by 51 feet almost matched the Methodist one, and although the old walls were used, the windows were enlarged and shuttered. The floor was laid with flagstones, galleries and pews were newly constructed, and the pulpit was given a classic accent with a Greek key design. The church as we see it now looks as nearly like that of 1850 as its congregation could make it in the restoration completed in 1944.[43] The interior was refurbished; the original oil lamps which had been scattered through other buildings in Fincastle were brought back and rehung. The Greek pulpit had been given to a local Negro congregation, which in turn had passed it on to their town hall, but a copy of the pulpit, slightly larger, was made and installed, and the railing in front of it was restored. The Sunday School hall at the back of the church was built in 1957.

By mid-nineteenth century, then, Fincastle had assumed its present aspect; its white steeples rising above the trees and rooftops were the first notes to catch the eye of any visitor approaching the town. We may well imagine with what pride the little community exhibited, as it still does, its courthouse and churches. They bore the mark of fashionable styles, but they were essentially discreet, conservative as Fincastle taste has always been.

And, as we might expect, most Fincastle families showed equal discretion in building new homes as the decades passed. Generally they preferred the accepted, practical, and tasteful simplicity of the old forms: a rectangle with one or two rooms on either side of a central hall,

[41] *Herald*, February 1, 1894.   [42] Stoner, p. 359.
[43] Frances McNulty Logan, "The Church's One Foundation," *Garden Gossip*, January, 1945; *Roanoke Times*, September 9, 1944.

sometimes a wing to the rear, end chimneys, neatly but not elaborately cut wooden paneling for walls, staircases, mantelpieces. Some used the Valley of Virginia narrow one- or two-story porches at front center.

Still in use in Fincastle and its environs are many such houses built before the war years, usually now remodeled and sometimes with their

25   Presbyterian Church after Enlargement in 1849

original appearance considerably changed.[44] One is the Hedrick house opposite the Methodist Church, another the Kent B. Stoner (now the Trigg) house on Carper Street. A mile or so north of Fincastle is a more elaborate example in brick, the house called Willoma, on the present Compton property, which has the double-storied porch. A mile southeast stands the farmhouse originally called Oakland, remodeled by its owners, the Muse family. Behind this are an old slave graveyard and a spring.

A special type of building of which one example exists in Fincastle is a springhouse, built directly over the water source (as were some of the pioneer log houses). This one, on the Peck property on the west side of town, is thought to date from the 1840's. There were then two rooms on the ground level, one enclosing the spring and the other used for storage, and there were living quarters on the second floor. The section on the west side has been added to the first log structure. (Such springhouses were sometimes more elaborate; one built of brick, with five rooms and a large fireplace on the exterior, still exists on the Crumpacker property in nearby Cloverdale.)

Two of the more elegant homes have been lost to us. One was the Anderson home called Montrose in northeast Fincastle, built in 1836 and destroyed in the 1930's. Here a classical note appeared in the large columns supporting the porch roof, a change from the familiar double-storied porch scheme. The other was the Preston house, Greenfield, to which a new wing in Greek Revival style had been added about 1840.

But the brick Breckenridge house on the corner of Main and Hancock Streets, built by Captain Sam Figgatt before 1840, illustrates one variation of Classical style. This is the simplified, flexible treatment of the Classic which is often called the "Tuscan idiom" and which is a free adaptation of the Italian villa style popular in mid-century. The rather severe look of the big blocks of the structure, its spare cornice and windows, is lightened by projecting bay windows and porches. The once separate kitchen has been connected to the house by a bricked-in passageway, and the woodwork of the porches suggests that they were rebuilt later in the century. But within are still the high-ceilinged parlors and bedrooms, well lighted by rectangular panels over inner doors. (Outside of Fincastle there was a magnificent house in this style

[44] Information about homes and business establishments mentioned in the following paragraphs comes from owners, from Fincastle residents, and, for the Bruce-Hurt house, from Mr. Marshall Harris, manager of Woodrum Field.

on a farm which occupied the site of the present Roanoke airport. This house, begun by Alexander Bruce in 1854 and finished by John W. Hurt in 1860, was the finest example of an Italian villa anywhere in the vicinity. Its builder was a man named Deyerle. The structure was razed in 1954 for airport development.)

Probably built in the decades before the war were several structures clustered in the clearing around the town spring. South of the spring stood a log market house (its site is shown on the map of 1880), a place where much horse, cattle, and hog trading went on. Close by this was a slaughterhouse where many of the "drove hogs" were butchered, and a tannery or two were there also. That portion of Back Street which rises to the east of the spring used to be called Jockey Alley because of the horse trading there. Perhaps in this area were already the coffin shop (one is advertised in an 1881 newspaper by J. Carleton Simpson, Carpenter and Undertaker),[45] and the stave mill, offering items such as pick handles and wagon spokes. These stood at the base of the hill on which rises the Presbyterian Church.

By 1860 Fincastle had a population of 876 as against the 703 of 1835, and the town took an active part in the war.[46] One of the twelve Botetourt companies engaged in combat was called the Fincastle Rifles. The mills provided wool for uniforms, and wagons, saddles, and harnesses were supplied by Fincastle manufacturers. The war did not alter the aspect of Fincastle, but disastrous fires did—one in 1870 and another in 1871; many buildings were destroyed in the western end of town. Among these were the "Gunger Shop," which sold its ginger-bread and cakes half a block down Main Street from the courthouse, the first office of the *Fincastle Herald*, dry-goods stores, drugstores, saloons, and offices. Several of these wooden buildings were replaced by brick ones in the next decades.

In 1880 a new map of Fincastle was printed by Gray and Son of Philadelphia. This shows expansion of the town to east, south, and west, and 184 lots are noted, in contrast to the 103 drawn in 1822. The population figure, however, had gone down to 675. It was to rise, though, during the summer months—and this rising brings another chapter in the history of the town.

[45] *Herald*, June 9, 1881.
[46] For population figures and for information on Fincastle's activities during the war years, see Irwin B. Cohen and others, *An Economic and Social Survey of Botetourt County* (University of Virginia, School of Rural Social Economics; Charlottesville, Va., 1942), pp. 18ff., 51.

FINCASTLE SPRINGS

III

Our name is widely known:
Far, far away, and from a warmer zone
Fair tourists come with spirits high and gay—
And come to stay!

This is our lasting wealth:
The mineral water, and the bracing air,
The long romantic drives with tonic rare,
Imparting health.

So read two of the stanzas in an eloquent testimonial poem by Fanny Johnston which appeared in the *Fincastle Herald* in 1885. Although Fincastle was on one of the routes leading to the famed Virginia spas of the nineteenth century—one of the earliest stones in the Presbyterian graveyard bears the sad note of the death of Mrs. Maria Pollock, wife of a Savannah physician, who, "in attempting a weary and painful journey to the Springs, to alleviate Pulmonary Consumption," died at Fincastle on August 7, 1814[1]—it was not until the end of that century that Fincastle itself became a mecca for health seekers.

But it had a brief blossoming in the 1880's and 1890's, with a hundred

[1] Rev. J. M. Holladay, *A Partial History of Fincastle Presbyterian Church* (Richmond, Va., 1902), p. 28.

or more visitors coming annually from such far-off points as New Orleans, Baton Rouge, and Opelousas; Vicksburg, Macon, Florence, and Mobile; St. Louis, Galveston, and Houston. Their names and the accounts of their activities filled the social columns of the *Herald* in the summer months. Fincastle's climate, scenery, and the hospitality of its people, as a writer for the *Herald* mentions, combined to make it "one of the most desirable 'retreats' in the mountains of Virginia."[2]

But it was the discovery of mineral waters which provided the stimulus needed to attract to Fincastle the "refined and intelligent society" of the summer boarders. And very special mineral waters they were: the only ferromagnesian springs as yet discovered on the continent. Samples were sent to be exhibited at the Chicago World's Fair of 1893 (along with a machine for wrapping oranges, by E. T. Nininger of Daleville.)[3] One could of course buy the bottled water—"Nature's Great Health Restorer" reads the *Herald* advertisement—it could be delivered by railroad at five dollars for a case of one dozen half-gallon bottles (and "Ministers of the Gospel will only be charged cost of shipment").[4] But how much pleasanter to drink it in company in a cooler climate, to stroll to the springs in the intervals between other diversions!

The little springhouse stands on the Mill Creek Church Road less than a mile east of town, in a narrow valley between winding hills. The hexagonal canopy with latticework trim, somewhat battered now and its stone base hidden by weeds and briars, is picturesque still. One can easily imagine how attractive a note it must have been in this landscape three-quarters of a century ago.

The railroad which shipped the Fincastle Mineral Water could not bring visitors directly into town (Fanny Johnston's poem admits

> we must confess
> The railroad came just near enough to slay
> Our trade with Troutville six miles away)

but they could make connections with the trains of the Atlantic, Mississippi and Ohio Railroad at Bonsack's depot. Arriving at Bonsack's at 5 P.M., they could transfer to a stagecoach running daily that would get them to Fincastle at 8:30, and the fare (in 1881) was only a dollar

---

[2] *Herald*, August 2, 1894. All succeeding notes, unless otherwise noted, are from the *Herald*.
[3] September 1, 1892.   [4] January 15, 1885.

and a half, with a fifty-cent reduction for a round-trip ticket. William B. Hayth was the agent at Fincastle; naturally the stage office was at his hotel near the courthouse.[5]

In 1881 there were two main hotels. The older was the Western, built after the great fire of 1870, which had started in its stables. Its wooden units were replaced by brick ones which may still be seen behind the courthouse (they are now owned by C. V. Dodd). In 1881 these were leased from Hayth by J. W. McCormick.

McCormick's public notice in the *Herald* shows him ready for trade:

WESTERN HOTEL
Fincastle, Va.

Having leased the above hotel I am prepared
to accommodate the public on terms to
Suit the Times!
Board by the month as reasonable as elsewhere.
Stock fed and Sale Stable kept in connection
with the house. Also a first-class BAR will
be kept in connection with the house, of
purest wines and whiskies.[6]

A few years earlier Hayth had bought a boardinghouse on the site of the old Nece Union Hotel and Craft tavern and had converted it into a thirty-bed hotel. The balconied structure of this original Hayth's House is still in use, as is a later wooden annex to the right on Roanoke Street (the W. B. Crush property). Besides the summer visitors, lawyers too had patronized the hotel, stepping across the street from the row of brick offices which stood behind the courthouse.

Hayth's advertisement of 1881 is a bit more restrained than McCormick's:

HAYTH'S HOUSE
Roanoke Street near Court House
Fincastle   Virginia

I am prepared to offer to the public the
accommodations of a FIRST-CLASS HOUSE. The
table furnished with the best of the season;
also good attention given to horses. I
respectfully ask a share of the public patronage.[7]

[5] June 9, 1881.   [6] *Idem.*   [7] *Idem.*

But he became the big hotel manager, for by January of 1882 he was running both hotels:

NEW COMBINED HOTEL!

In Fincastle

Having taken charge of the Western Hotel in
Fincastle, I shall keep hereafter Hayth's
Hotel and the Western Hotel together as one
house, and will give my own attention to
them, and will guarantee a

FIRST CLASS HOUSE

to the public. The table supplied with the
best of the season. Stables well filled.
BAR ROOM at each house filled with the best

LIQUORS, WINES, CIGARS, Etc.

Thankful for past patronage I ask a
continuance of the same.

LARGE SAMPLE ROOM

for Commercial men always ready.[8]

By the summer of 1894 Fincastle was "quite a lively town," and Hayth's Hotel was "filled to full capacity since the opening of the season" with "nearly if not quite one hundred boarders," according to the social notes in the newspaper, "and those stopping at private homes will probably swell the total number to a hundred and forty."[9] This was a sizable number of visitors for a town with a population of 675 or fewer. In 1894 an addition was made to the Western of a large dining room with lodging rooms above.[10]

Ready for the summer trade in 1895 was a larger addition to Hayth's eastern section, erected by Gratton T. Firebaugh, contractor. This was a three-story structure with its entire first floor, 32 by 56 feet, serving as a music hall (an older music hall now became a sample room). Eight bedrooms with "12 feet pitch" were lined up on each upper floor along the eight-foot-wide hallway which ran the entire length of the building, as did the balconies "which afford splendid views of landscape and mountain scenery."[11] Unfortunately this section of the hotel no longer exists.

We can, however, form some picture of the activities of these

[8] September 7, 1882; the advertisement is signed by Hayth and dated January 19.
[9] August 2 and 30, 1894.   [10] March 22, 1894.   [11] March 7, 1895.

summers. The "most brilliant social event" of the 1894 summer season was a "Mother Goose party" given in Hayth's ballroom, which was beautifully decorated with ferns and garlands of evergreens. The dominant New Orleans contingent took over. Miss Mary Young had suggested the theme, Mrs. Valades played the piano, and Mrs. Girault impersonated Mother Goose. Dancing began at 8 P.M. and continued until long past midnight, with diversions, chief of which was the awarding of prizes. Miss Loretta McEnany, also of New Orleans, won a live goose as a first prize for her costume of Little Bo-Peep, and Peachy Breckenridge of Fincastle, who came as Little Boy Blue, won the gentlemen's first prize, a stuffed alligator.[12]

Other gala affairs occurred almost weekly: donkey parties, phantom balls, germans. Also there were musicales, with duets and choruses vying with vocal, instrumental, and whistling solos. Sometimes, especially before Hayth built the new music hall in the hotel, these were held in the courthouse across the street; we can imagine the gaily dressed ladies flirting with their escorts under its handsome columned portico. Held at the courthouse was the World's Fair Concert in late August of 1892, when Miss Melanie Holt of Galveston was encored for her sweet rendering of a Spanish air, "La Paloma."[13]

Occasionally, too, summer guests were invited to a ball or to a picnic party at Grove Hill, the magnificent Breckenridge mansion in nearby Catawba.[14] If they wanted to go further afield, they could hire delivery teams and visit the Natural Bridge, the Peaks of Otter (from which they saw the lights of Roanoke), or the White Rock and Flowing Spring, or make the extended trip to one of the famous springs, Warm, White Sulphur, or Old Sweet.[15] Gentlemen interested in politics may have been drawn to Roanoke by the announcement in the *Herald* on September 22, 1892, which mentioned that the "Hon. Adlai A. Stevenson, of Illinois, the Democratic candidate for Vice-President," was to speak there the following Monday; "he draws large crowds wherever he appears." Ladies interested in new fashions need not go afield, for right in the hotel was Mrs. S. E. Hayth's millinery shop with its new styles imported from Richmond, Baltimore, and New York.[16]

By walking a block or two from Hayth's Hotel, summer visitors could admire the newer houses on Roanoke and Main Streets. The streets themselves were still unpaved, but rows of steppingstones were placed

[12] August 2, 1894.   [13] September 1, 1892; August 16, 23, September 20, 1894.
[14] August 30, 1894.   [15] July 26, August 9, 1894.   [16] June 9, 1881.

across their intersections, as we can see in old photographs of the town. The *Herald* commented in June of 1881 on John N. Slicer's new home, just then finished: "one of the prettiest in town," with "a good deal of fancy work about it."[17] There was less fancy work but instead a sober elegance in two of the houses newly built in the "Tuscan villa" manner already mentioned. One was the Beckley house at 21 Roanoke Street, finished in 1875 as a residence for Brown M. Allen, then clerk of Botetourt County,[18] and the other Captain Jim Figgatt's (now the Graybill-Woltz) house, at 20 Main Street, built in 1880.[19] The pairs of tall narrow windows, the bracketed cornice, the porch, and the bay window at the side of the Beckley house are all typical of the style. The Figgatt house exhibits a somewhat more austere version, especially since the porch which originally extended across the front has been in part removed. Notable here are the sturdy 18-inch-thick brick outer walls, the high-ceilinged rooms, and the imported marble fireplaces in two of the first-floor drawing rooms. Another attractive home which dates from this period is the Godwin cottage, on the other side of town near the spring.

Some of the New Orleans visitors may have left their mark on the architecture of the town. It is said, for example, that the New Orleans bride of one of the owners of the Price (now Waid) house, built in the 1870's across from Captain Figgatt's, had all its ceilings raised and added wrought-iron balconies on front and sides. This charming house, remodeled again in a more recent decade, is quite elaborate in surface decoration, and the central hall utilizes curves both in its ground plan and in its graceful hanging staircase. But it reflects still the old Valley of Virginia scheme in its plan and its double-storied porch.

Several commercial buildings were erected in these years, notably in the area around the courthouse. The new building for the *Fincastle Herald* office, still in existence, was completed in January of 1894, with brick replacing a frame structure destroyed by fire several months before.[20] The Luster store, finished in July of 1894, drew admiring comment from the newspaper:

The iron and brick front of Mr. J. O. Luster's tin and stove establishment on Roanoke Street is very pretty and attractive, and is naturally the subject of favorable comment by our people. Iron cornice and window capping adorn the front, making a pretty combination with

[17] *Idem.*   [18] April 9, 1964.   [19] Information from Mrs. Rosco Woltz.
[20] January 25, 1894.

26   *The Jail*

the neatly stained and pencilled brickwork. Mr. Luster evidently has an eye for the beautiful as well as the substantial, and deserves the thanks of our people in helping, at an unnecessary expense, to improve the appearance of the town. His is an example that is worthy of emulation.[21]

Actually Luster's store was outclassed in 1897, when the county jail was erected next to the courthouse, under the direction of the contractor S. L. Rice.[22] The jail, of red brick, was small, 32 feet on each side, and rose three stories above the basement. The first floor was divided into four rooms serving as an apartment for the jailer. The second floor held a room for the sheriff, a search room and bath, and four cells, and the third floor was simply one large room with six cells opening from a central corridor. But on the exterior the jail is by far the most ornate building of this period in Fincastle. Again there may have been some Deep-South influence in the delightfully decorative ironwork of its balcony, the gaiety of which masks the use of up-to-date steel plate jail cells and roof, and the fireproof walls within.

Such use of modern materials might seem to presage a new age of modern building in the town, but actually it did not, although there were hopes earlier in the 1880's for expansion of the town and a boom in building. Fincastle's population in 1880 totaled 675; for four or five decades it had been decreasing and an influx of a hundred or more visitors yearly had considerable impact. Fanny Johnston's poem of 1885 was titled "A Retrospect and a Prophecy"; she reminds us that "In antebellum years she [Fincastle] reached her prime," but she also reflects the hopes of the mid-80's. These were of the coming railroad ("The iron horse shall neigh upon her streets") and of the expansion of town and industry.

On May 21, 1892, the *Herald* told its readers that "The Botetourt Development Company has lately broken ground for a railroad, which is to connect with the Shenandoah Valley Railroad at or near Cloverdale," and on July 7 it reported a visit by Captain Hathaway, secretary-treasurer of the Roanoke, Fincastle and Clifton Forge Railroad, which was to be connected with the Chesapeake and Ohio at Eagle Rock. Captain Hathaway admitted that workers were scarce but were coming in and spoke hopefully of the early completion of this road.

Meanwhile a Fincastle Land and Improvement Company had been formed to enlarge the town south and east of its existing limits. A map

[21] August 2, 1894.   [22] April 1, 1897.

showing the property of the company, 468 acres in all, was completed by a Mr. Thayer and commented on in the *Herald* on May 21, 1891. That the summer visitors played an important part in these plans is evident in the newspaper report, which speaks particularly of a projected new railroad hotel. This was to have been an enlargement of the lovely old mansion Santillane; that name was to be used for the hotel, and a Santillane Avenue was to intersect with old Catawba Avenue (the present route 220): "On the property this hotel occupies a splendid place, on a slight eminence, and when the splendid building now there will have been enlarged and converted into a magnificent new hotel it will be one of the loveliest and most interesting places in Virginia for the summer visitor and tourist."

A passenger station and the main line of the Roanoke, Fincastle and Clifton Forge Railway were also delineated.[23] Streets and avenues were laid out. Four of these bore the names of the company's officers: President R. T. Herndon, Vice-President C. H. Vines, Secretary R. L.

[23] Information about the map is taken from an article by Raymond Colley published in the *Roanoke Times*, September 30, 1951.

27   View of Fincastle from Prospect

Housman, and Treasurer James Godwin, but others apparently honored the summer guests with streets named Charleston, Houston, and Texas. Building lots had been surveyed, and a factory site was located at the western border of town. "Santillane Park" and "villa sites" were placed at the southeast and bordered by a street named Frisco Place. The newspaper writer's enthusiasm for all this was tempered, and he ended his account on a rather nostalgic note: "The idea then suggests itself that it is a pity to convert such a pretty place into town lots, but sentiment must give way to progress in these booming times."

Expansion and boom, however, did not come. Summer visitors dwindled in number and finally stopped coming to Fincastle. The real-estate scheme failed for lack of investors, and only Herndon Street remains to commemorate it. The railway never materialized beyond the making of a few stretches of roadbed, and even a projected trolley line failed. Nor did any new industry enter to change the pattern of the town.

Fincastle remains a small quiet community rooted in the past. There is no great variety of architectural styles within the town, but conservatism here shows taste and discretion, and the total effect is one of great charm. Even the twentieth-century visitor can grasp some of the character and personality which determined the life and growth of Fincastle and keep a vivid memory of its pleasant homes, its peaceful streets, and its white steeples rising against a frame of low wooded Virginia hills.

INDEX

THE TOWN OF FINCASTLE, VIRGINIA

was composed, printed, and bound by
Kingsport Press, Inc., Kingsport, Tennessee.
The map is from the
County Courthouse in Fincastle
and was reproduced by
The Reynolds Co., Charlottesville, Virginia.
The paper is Mohawk Superfine, and the
types are Caledonia and Scotch Roman.
Designed by Edward Foss.